Practical
Pre-School

D0247985

Planning
for Learning
through

All About Me

Rachel Sparks Linfield and Penny Coltman Illustrated by Cathy Hughes

Contents

Published by Step Forward Publishing Limited
25 Cross Street, Leamington Spa, CV32 4PX   Tel: 01926 420046   www.practicalpreschool.com
© Step Forward Publishing Limited 2001

Planning for Learning through All About Me ISBN: 1 902438 41 8

Making plans

Why plan?

The purpose of planning is to make sure that all children enjoy a broad and balanced curriculum. All planning should be useful. Plans are working documents which you spend time preparing, but which should later repay your efforts. Try to be concise. This will help you in finding information quickly when you need it.

Long-term plans

Preparing a long-term plan, which maps out the curriculum during a year or even two, will help you to ensure that you are providing a variety of activities and are meeting the statutory requirements of the *Curriculum Guidance for the Foundation Stage* (2000).

Your long-term plan need not be detailed. Divide the time period over which you are planning into fairly equal sections, such as half terms. Choose a topic for each section. Young children benefit from making links between the new ideas they encounter so as you select each topic, think about the time of year in which you plan to do it. A topic about minibeasts will not be very successful in November!

Although each topic will address all the learning areas, some could focus on a specific area. For example, a topic on All About Me lends itself well to activities relating to Personal, Social and Emotional Development and Knowledge and Understanding of the World. Another topic might particularly encourage the appreciation of stories. Try to make sure that you provide a variety of topics in your long-term plans.

Autumn 1	All About Me
Autumn 2	Autumn/Christmas
Spring 1	Fairy Stories
Spring 2	Colour
Summer 1	Toys
Summer 2	Minibeasts

Medium-term plans

Medium-term plans will outline the contents of a topic in a little more detail. One way to start this process is by brainstorming on a large piece of paper. Work with your team writing down all the activities you can think of which are relevant to the topic. As you do this it may

become clear that some activities go well together. Think about dividing them into themes. All About Me, for example, has themes such as 'Hands', 'Looking', 'Listening' and 'Faces'.

At this stage it is helpful to make a chart. Write the theme ideas down the side of the chart and put a different area of learning at the top of each column. Now you can insert your brainstormed ideas and quickly see where there are gaps. As you complete the chart take account of children's earlier experiences and provide opportunities for them to progress.

Refer back to the *Curriculum Guidance for the Foundation Stage* (2000) and check that you have addressed as many different aspects as you can. Once all your medium-term plans are complete make sure that there are no neglected areas.

Day-to-day plans

The plans you make for each day will outline aspects such as:

- resources needed;
- the way in which you might introduce activities;
- the organisation of adult help;
- size of the group;
- timing.

Making plans

stretched over a longer period or condensed to meet the needs of any group. You will almost certainly adapt the activities as children respond to them in different ways and bring their own ideas, interests and enthusiasms. The important thing is to ensure that the children are provided with a varied and enjoyable curriculum which meets their individual developing needs.

Using the book

- Collect or prepare suggested resources as listed on page 21.

- Read the section which outlines links to the Early Learning Goals (pages 4 - 7) and explains the rationale for the topic of All About Me.

- For each weekly theme two activities are described in detail as an example to help you in your planning and preparation. Key vocabulary, questions and learning opportunities are identified.

- The skills chart on page 23 will help you to see at a glance which aspects of children's development are being addressed as a focus each week.

- As children take part in the All About Me topic activities, their learning will progress. 'Collecting evidence' on page 22 explains how you might monitor children's achievements.

- Find out on page 20 how the topic can be brought together in a grand finale involving parents, children and friends.

- There is additional material to support the working partnership of families and children in the form of a 'Home links' page, and a photocopiable 'Parent's page' found at the back of the book.

It is important to appreciate that the ideas presented in this book will only be a part of your planning. Many activities which will be taking place as routine in your group may not be mentioned. For example, it is assumed that sand, dough, water, puzzles, floor toys and large scale apparatus are part of the ongoing pre-school experience. Many groups will also be able to provide access to computers and other aspects of information and communication technology. Role play areas, stories, rhymes and singing, and group discussion times are similarly assumed to be happening each week although they may not be a focus for described activities.

Identify the learning which each activity is intended to promote. Make a note of any assessments or observations that you are likely to carry out. On your plans make notes of which activities were particularly successful, or any changes you would make another time.

A final note

Planning should be seen as flexible. Not all groups meet every day, and not all children attend every day. Any part of the plan can be used independently,

Using the Early Learning Goals

Having decided on your topic and made your medium-term plans you can use the Early Learning Goals to highlight the key learning opportunities your activities will address. The Early Learning Goals are split into six areas: Personal, Social and Emotional Development; Communication, Language and Literacy; Mathematical Development; Knowledge and Understanding of the World; Physical Development and Creative Development. Do not expect each of your topics to cover every goal but your long-term plans should allow for each child to work towards all of the goals.

The following section highlights parts of the *Curriculum Guidance for the Foundation Stage* (2000) in point form to show what children are expected to be able to do in each area of learning by the time they enter Year 1. These points will be used throughout this book to show how activities for a topic on All About Me link to these expectations. For example, Personal, Social and Emotional Development point 8 is 'work as part of a group or class taking turns'. Activities suggested which provide the opportunity for children to do this will have the reference PS8. This will enable you to see which parts of the Early Learning Goals are covered in a given week and plan for areas to be revisited and developed.

In addition you can ensure that activities offer variety in the outcomes to be encountered. Often a similar activity may be carried out to achieve different outcomes. For example, during this topic children make an eye colour bar chart. They will be saying and using number names but they will also be using language such as 'more' and 'fewer', collaborating and learning to work together. It is important therefore that activities have clearly defined learning outcomes so that these may be emphasised during the activity and for recording purposes.

Personal, Social and Emotional Development (PS)

This area of learning incorporates attitudes, skills and understanding and is a pre-condition for children's success in all other learning. The goals include children's personal, social, emotional, moral and spiritual development and the establishment of good attitudes to their learning.

By the end of the Foundation Stage most children will:

PS1 continue to be interested, excited and motivated to learn

PS2 be confident to try activities, initiate ideas and speak in a familiar group

PS3 maintain attention, concentrate and sit quietly when appropriate

PS4 have a developing awareness of their own needs, views and feelings and be sensitive to the needs, views and feelings of others

PS5 have a developing respect for their own cultures and beliefs and those of other people

PS6 be responsive to significant experiences, showing a range of feelings when appropriate

PS7 form good relationships with peers and adults

PS8 work as a part of a group or class, taking turns and sharing fairly; understanding that there need to be agreed values and codes of behaviour for groups of people, including adults and children, to work harmoniously

PS9 understand what is right, what is wrong and why

PS10 dress and undress independently and manage their own personal hygiene

PS11 select and use activities and resources independently

PS12 consider the consequences of their words and actions for themselves and others

PS13 understand that people have different needs, views, cultures and beliefs which need to be treated with respect

PS14 understand that they can expect others to treat their needs, views, cultures and beliefs with respect

The topic of All About Me offers many opportunities for children's personal, social and emotional development. Time spent discussing the importance of various body parts will encourage children to speak in a group, to be interested and to consider consequences. By playing circle games children will learn to take turns and to understand the need for agreed codes of behaviour. Many of the areas outlined above, though, will be covered on an almost incidental basis as children carry out the activities described in this book for the other areas of learning. During undirected free choice times they will be developing PS11 whilst any small group activity which involves working with an adult will help children to work towards PS7.

Communication, Language and Literacy (L)

The objectives set out in the *National Literacy Stratagy: Framework for Teaching* for the reception year are in line with these goals. By the end of the Foundation Stage, most children will be able to:

L1 enjoy listening to and using spoken and written language, and readily turn to it in their play and learning

L2 explore and experiment with sounds, words and texts

L3 listen with enjoyment, and respond to stories, songs and other music, rhymes and poems and make up their own stories, songs, rhymes and poems

L4 use language to imagine and recreate roles and experiences

L5 use talk to organise, sequence and clarify thinking, ideas, feelings and events

L6 sustain attentive listening, responding to what they have heard by relevant comments, questions or actions

L7 interact with others, negotiating plans and activities and taking turns in conversation

L8 extend their vocabulary, exploring the meaning and sounds of new words

L9 retell narratives in the correct sequence, drawing on language patterns of stories

L10 speak clearly and audibly with confidence and control and show awareness of the listener, for example by their use of conventions such as greetings, 'please' and 'thank you'

L11 hear and say initial and final sounds in words, and short vowel sounds within words

L12 link sounds to letters, naming and sounding letters of the alphabet

L13 read a range of familiar and common words and simple sentences independently

L14 show an understanding of the elements of stories such as main character, sequence of events, and openings and how information can be found in non-fiction texts to answer questions about where, who, why and how

L15 know that print carries meaning and, in English, is read from left to right and top to bottom

L16 attempt writing for different purposes, using features of different forms such as lists, stories and instructions

L17 write their own names and other things such as labels and captions, and begin to form simple sentences, sometimes using punctuation

L18 use their phonic knowledge to write simple regular words and make phonetically plausible attempts at more complex words

L19 use a pencil and hold it effectively to form recognisable letters, most of which are correctly formed

The activities suggested for the theme of All About Me include several which are based on well-known, quality picture books and stories. They allow children to enjoy listening to the books and to respond in a variety of ways to what they hear, reinforcing and extending their vocabularies. Throughout the topic opportunities are described in which children are encouraged to explore the sounds of words, to use descriptive vocabulary and to see some of their ideas recorded in both pictures and words. As children become more aware of their hands, their eyes and their ears they are encouraged to use their senses during story times, role-play situations and book-making activities.

Mathematical Development (M)

The objectives set out in the *National Numeracy Strategy: Framework for Teaching* for the reception year are in line with these goals. By the end of the Foundation Stage, most children will be able to:

M1 say and use number names in order in familiar contexts

M2 count reliably up to ten everyday objects;

M3 recognise numerals 1 to 9

M4 use language such as 'more' or 'less' to compare two numbers

M5 in practical activities and discussion begin to use the vocabulary involved in adding and subtracting

M6 find one more or one less than a number from one to ten

M7 begin to relate addition to combining two groups of objects and subtraction to 'taking away'

M8 talk about, recognise and recreate simple patterns

M9 use language such as 'circle' or 'bigger' to describe the shape and size of solids and flat shapes

M10 use everyday words to describe position

M11 use developing mathematical ideas and methods to solve practical problems

M12 use language such as 'greater', 'smaller', 'heavier' or 'lighter' to compare quantities

The theme of All About Me provides a meaningful context for mathematical activities. Children are given the opportunity to count people, hands and facial features and to begin to develop language for addition and subtraction. Hands and feet are used as non-standard units for measuring. There are opportunities for children to explore shape, size and position as they compare ears and hands whilst the 'Listening week' allows children to play a variety of lotto type number games.

Knowledge and Understanding of the World (K)

These goals provide a foundation for scientific, technological, historical and geographical learning.

By the end of the Foundation Stage most children will be able to:

K1 investigate objects and materials by using all of their senses as appropriate

K2 find out about and identify some features of living things, objects and events they observe

K3 look closely at similarities, differences, patterns and change

K4 ask questions about why things happen and how things work

K5 build and construct with a wide range of objects, selecting appropriate resources and adapting their work where necessary

K6 select tools and techniques they need to shape, assemble and join the materials they are using

K7 find out about and identify the uses of everyday technology and use communication technology and programmable toys to support their learning

K8 find out about past and present events in their own lives, and in those of their families and other people they know

K9   observe, find out about and identify features in the place they live and the natural world

K10   begin to know about their own cultures and beliefs and those of other people

K11   find out about their environment and talk about those features they like and dislike

The topic of All About Me offers many opportunities for children to make observations, to ask questions and to compare. They can explore the differences and similarities in eyes, hands, feet and ears. By making jointed bodies and a full sized poster of a child they will become more aware of their own bodies and how the various parts are positioned. By recording finger prints with chalk/ink and hand prints in clay, and by making face masks they will be encouraged to notice details and features whilst at the same time gain a greater understanding of the properties of materials.

Physical Development (PD)

By the end of the Foundation Stage most children will be able to:

PD1   move with confidence, imagination and in safety

PD2   move with control and co-ordination

PD3   show awareness of space, of themselves and of others

PD4   recognise the importance of keeping healthy and those things which contribute to this

PD5   recognise the changes that happen to their bodies when they are active

PD6   use a range of small and large equipment

PD7   travel around, under, over and through balancing and climbing equipment

PD8   handle tools, objects, construction and malleable materials safely with increasing control.

Activities such as playing with playdough and construction toys with small pieces will offer experience of PD8. Through pretending to be spies in disguise shadowing a person or by playing 'Keeper of the keys' children will have the opportunity to develop PD1 and 2. As children learn how to warm up before active games they will become more aware of how their bodies change. As children are encouraged to notice what their bodies can do there are many opportunities for aiming, balancing and movement activities.

Creative Development (C)

By the end of the Foundation Stage most children will be able to:

C1   explore colour, texture, shape, form and space in two or three dimensions

C2   listen attentively to and explore how sounds can be made louder/quieter, faster/slower, longer/shorter, higher/lower and recognise patterns in music, movement and dance

C3   respond in a variety of ways to what they see, hear, smell, touch and feel

C4   use their imagination in art and design, music, dance, imaginative and role play and stories

C5   express and communicate their ideas, thoughts and feelings by using a widening range of materials, suitable tools, imaginative and role play, movement, designing and making, and a variety of songs and musical instruments

During this topic children will experience working with a variety of materials as they make collages of faces and clown puppets. They will be able to develop their skills of painting and colour mixing as they paint self-portraits and so work towards C1 and 4. A number of songs which have body parts in them have been suggested which could also have actions and percussion added, so allowing children to use their imagination in music. Throughout all the activities children are encouraged to talk about what they see and feel as they communicate their ideas in painting, collage work and role play.

Week 1

Bits and pieces

Personal, Social and Emotional Development

- During circle time show children how to roll a ball gently to a friend. On receiving the ball the child says 'My name is _____ and with my * I can _____.' The * should be a body part such as 'with my hands I can draw'. (PS3, 8)

- Make a collection of objects familiar to the children which can be used in a foot feely box. Children should take it in turns to feel an object with their feet and describe it to the rest of the group. After the game has finished, talk about whether it is easier to use feet or hands for this activity and why. (PS2, 8)

- Use a large picture of a child as the focus for a discussion on body parts and how useful they are. For example, the nose can smell and act as a filter for dust and smoke particles. (PS2, 3, 6)

Communication, Language and Literacy

- Read *Funnybones* by Janet and Allan Ahlberg (Puffin Books). Talk about skeletons and how they support our bodies. Re-read the story encouraging children to join in. (L3, 5, 6)

- Help children to write name labels for a display of self-portraits. (L17, 19)

- Take a photograph of each child. Mount each one on a large sheet of card and ask each child to complete a page about themselves for a big book. Each page should give the child's name, their age, what they like to do and any other details which fit in with the body 'bits and pieces' theme. (L19)

Mathematical Development

- Help children to draw round their feet. Compare feet sizes and use them as a non-standard measure for a variety of lengths. (M12)

- Use *Funnybones* by Janet and Allan Ahlberg (Puffin Books) as the stimulus for comparing sizes of dolls and teddies and to reinforce associated language for size. (M12)

- Play a Beetle drive type game in which children throw a dice and each number corresponds to a part of the body. (M3)

Knowledge and Understanding of the World

- Draw around a child. Label different parts of the body (see activity opposite). (K2)

- Make skeletons from pieces of white paper straws mounted on black paper. (K5)

- To reinforce names of body parts make jointed people from card pieces with brass fasteners for the joints. (K2, 5)

Physical Development

- Play 'Simon says', emphasising names of body parts in the instructions. (PD 1, 2)

- Experiment with travelling and balancing using different body parts. (PD1, 2, 7)

- Play with balls and compare the way they move when they are thrown and kicked. Which parts of our bodies can we use to make the ball move? (PD6)

Creative Development

- Sing 'Heads, shoulders, knees and toes'. (C4)

- Paint self-portraits (see activity opposite). (C1)

- Explore which parts of the body can be used to make sounds to accompany songs. Children could clap, tap, click fingers, sniff, whistle, stamp, slap thighs, tap teeth, and so on. Encourage children to explore how the sounds can be made louder, quieter, faster and slower. (C2, 5)

Activity: Self-portraits

Learning opportunity: Painting based on close observation.

Early Learning Goal: Creative Development. Children will be able to explore colour and shape in two dimensions.

Resources: Ready-mixed paints in a range of colours so that children can pick the appropriate skin, hair and eye colours; plastic mirrors; photographs of people familiar to the group.

Key vocabulary: Names of colours, parts of the body, portrait.

Organisation: Small group.

What to do:

Show children the photographs. Who are in the photos? What are the people wearing? What colours are their hair? Show children the paints. Pick one person in the photos. Ask the group which paint they would choose for that person's hair if they were to do a portrait. What would they use for the skin? Explain to the children that they are going to paint self-portraits. Talk about the need to choose colours carefully so that everyone will be able to recognise them from the pictures. As children paint, encourage them to notice where eyes should be positioned, and how arms and legs are placed in relationship to their bodies.

Activity: Labelling body parts

Learning opportunity: Recognising and labelling parts of the body.

Early Learning Goal: Knowledge and Understanding of the World. Children will be able to find out about and identify some features of living things.

Resources: Large plain paper as long as a child; thick, black wax crayon; labels of the body parts.

Key vocabulary: Eye, ear, mouth, nose, head, arm, neck, elbow, hand, shoulder, tummy/stomach, waist, knee, foot, finger, toe (**Note:** The number and type of words to be used will vary from group to group.)

Organisation: Small group sitting on the floor.

What to do:

Introduce the activity with a quick game of 'Point to your ..... ' in order to assess which body part names children are already familiar with. Explain to the group that they are going to make a large poster to teach people the names for parts of the body. Show the children some of the labels. Can anyone recognise any of the words? What sounds do the words begin with? Choose a child who is wearing shorts or trousers to lie down on the large piece of paper and draw round with the wax crayon. Ask the children to help you stick the labels on to the poster. Mount the poster at floor height.

Display

Mount the body poster at floor height. As the weeks progress put out other labels for children to add to the body. Make a track of the feet used for measuring going to the body as if the body has walked all over the wall. Display the skeletons on a board near a table containing other books in the *Funnybones* series.

Cut around the portraits and mount on black sugar paper. Display the portraits against a background of a play area as if the children are enjoying a playtime together.

Week 2

Handy week

Personal, Social and Emotional Development

- During circle time play games in which children pass on claps of differing numbers and rhythms. Encourage children to listen and to take turns. (PS3, 8)

- Talk about the importance of washing hands before eating. Encourage children to become independent. (PS10)

- Talk about why people shake hands. Discuss which hand is shaken and reinforce 'right' and 'left'. For a week encourage children to shake hands with you each day when they arrive or before going home. (PS12)

Communication, Language and Literacy

- Clap children's names and encourage them to recognise their own and those of friends. (L1, 6)

- Prepare a feely bag of objects found in the classroom. Ask children to take it in turns to describe what they feel. (L6)

- Draw around children's hands and help them to fill their hands with either words or pictures of things they can do with their hands. Once full, cut them out. (L16, 19)

- Use fingers to enjoy practising early hand writing patterns in trays of coloured sand. (L19)

Mathematical Development

- Use a variety of finger rhymes to reinforce numbers to five. (M1)

- Use ready mixed paint to make a hand print for each child. When dry, cut around the prints and compare the sizes. Use the prints as leaves and ask the children to stick them on a large painted tree. Encourage the use of positional language as the children talk about where their 'leaves' have been stuck. (M10, 12)

- Measure lengths in hand spans. (M12)

- Play the handy estimation game (see activity opposite). (M4, 7)

Knowledge and Understanding of the World

- Make thumb prints. Use magnifiers to explore the different patterns and see how they are all different (see activity opposite). (K2, 3)

- Provide a range of materials for children to choose from to make their own models. As they work, encourage them to talk about what their hands are doing. (K5, 6)

- Compare hands. Help children to notice differences in palm lines, nail colours and sizes. Make a hand print in clay or dough. (K3)

Physical Development

- Encourage the development of fine motor skills by using construction toys with small pieces. (PD6)

- Play catching and throwing games. (PD6)

- Explore what hands can do to squeeze, roll and flatten playdough. (PD8)

Creative Development

- Use finger paints to make prints with fingers. Add lines and dots to turn the prints into small creatures. Encourage children to talk about their creatures. Where do they live? What can they do? What do they eat? (C4)

- Sing favourite songs and take it in turns to clap the rhythm. (C5)

- On black paper draw around a child's hand with white chalk several times so that the shapes touch and form a pattern. Ask children to choose three colours with which to paint their hand pattern. (C1)

Activity: Handy estimation game

Learning opportunity: Mathematical Development. Estimating and counting numbers to ten.

Early Learning Goal: Children will be able to count reliably up to ten everyday objects and use language such as 'more' and 'less' to compare two numbers.

Resources: A basket of small objects (for example, Unifix cubes) such that a child's handful would be no more than ten; number cards for numerals to nine.

Key vocabulary: Numbers to ten, more, less than, fewer.

Organisation: Small group.

What to do:

Invite a child to pick a handful of cubes from the basket. Ask the child to count how many there are. Ask another child to try and pick out a handful which has about the same number of cubes in it. How many are there? Is it the same number? Are there more/fewer cubes in the second handful? Continue this activity until all children have had a chance to be both the first picker and the second.

Next, show children a number card. Ask them to try to pick out quickly from the basket exactly the same number of cubes. Encourage children to do this by estimating rather than by counting. If appropriate, extend the game by asking children to pick up more/fewer cubes. On further occasions the language of addition/subtraction can also be used.

Activity: Thumb prints

Learning opportunity: Observing and describing thumb prints.

Early Learning Goal: Knowledge and Understanding of the World. Children will find out about and identify some features of living things, objects and events they observe. They will look closely at similarities, differences and patterns.

Resources: Wide sticky tape; scissors; white chalk; magnifiers; postcard sized pieces of black sugar paper.

Key vocabulary: Thumb, print.

Organisation: Small group.

What to do:

Explain to the children that everyone has thumb prints and that everybody's print is different. Ask the group to look at their thumb prints with the magnifiers. What can they see? Hand out pieces of white chalk and show the children how to cover their thumb prints with chalk dust. Being careful not to finger the sticky part of the tape, cut a piece and hold it firmly at each end. Ask a child to place their thumb in the centre on the sticky side and lift it off. Stick the tape on a piece of black sugar paper and let the child examine it. Repeat the sticky tape exercise for each child's left and right thumb, remembering to name each one. Help children to notice the different patterns and to draw what they see on white paper.

Display

Paint two large tree trunks with branches (let the children help you). Ask them where they want to stick their hand prints and handy words. Encourage them to explain the positions they choose rather than letting them simply point. On a nearby table place the clay hand prints and the thumb prints with two magnifiers.

Week 3
Listening week

Personal, Social and Emotional Development

- During circle time talk, about the importance of being a good listener. Emphasise that in order to show we are listening to someone we need to look at them as they speak. (PS3, 4)

- Tell the traditional tale of 'The boy who cried wolf'. Talk about the boy and why he should not have cried for help when he did not need it. (PS9)

- Make a collection of precious objects which make a sound, such as a china bell, a baby's rattle and a bunch of keys. Explain to the children why each object is precious. Talk about the need to handle precious objects with care. Do the group think they can pass them around so carefully that they will not make a sound? (PS4)

Communication, Language and Literacy

- Read *Peace at Last* by Jill Murphy (Macmillan Children's Books). Write a group version with new sounds (see activity opposite). (L3, 9, 15)

- Play Chinese whispers but instead of the final person saying the word they have heard, ask them to say the name of the letter or sound it begins with. (L6, 11)

- Begin a word bank of words which rhyme with 'ear'. (L8)

Mathematical Development

- Play number lotto and other games where children need to listen to instructions. (M1)

- Cut out a variety of different sizes and shapes of ears from card. Ask children to sort the ears according to shape and then to arrange each set in order of size. (M9)

- Provide each child with a small drum or shaker. Use these for counting activities. Ask children to shake/hit a given number of times. Ask them to count your taps/hits and to copy. Can they do one more hit? (M1, 6)

Knowledge and Understanding of the World

- Make a tape recording of each child saying 'Good morning'. Play the tape to the children. Can they identify their own voice? How does it compare to their normal speaking voice? (K3)

- Go on a sound detecting walk. (K2)

- Use a xylophone or glockenspiel to explore high and low notes. Invite children to design and make their own musical instruments and to describe the sounds they make. (K3, 6)

Physical Development

- Play games in which a whistle is blown or a drum is tapped a certain number of times to signify an action such as two taps means jump, one tap means hop and three taps means sit down. (PD1, 2, 3)

- Play 'The keeper of the keys' (see activity opposite). (PD2)

- Play musical statues, encouraging children to move in time with music and to stand still as soon as the music stops. Instead of asking children to sit out if they move after the music ends, praise those who remain still. (PD2, 3)

Creative Development

- Ask children to listen to extracts of *Peter and the Wolf*. Encourage children to make up dances to the music. (C5)

- Use *Peace at Last* by Jill Murphy or a similar book to which children can add percussion for sound effects. Tape record the story and sounds. Later use the tape as the stimulus for a music and movement session. (C4)

- Sing and make up actions for the song 'Do your ears hang low? in *Okki-tokki-unga Action Songs for Children* (A & C Black). (C5)

Activity: Peace at last

Learning opportunity: Collaborating to write and make a big book based on *Peace at Last*.

Early Learning Goal: Communication, Language and Literacy. Children will be able to retell narratives in the correct sequence, drawing on the language pattern of stories. They will attempt writing for different purposes.

Resources: *Peace at Last* (big book version if possible); large pieces of card or stiff paper for book pages; a variety of crayons, pencils and felt pens; a flip chart; a favourite doll or teddy owned by the group.

Key vocabulary: Vocabulary within *Peace at Last*, title, author.

Organisation: Whole group.

What to do:

At the beginning of the week read *Peace at Last* to the group. To introduce the writing of a big book, ask children to help retell the *Peace at Last* story by using the pictures in the book. Draw attention to details in the pictures and encourage all children to join in repeating phrases such as 'I can't stand this!'

Talk to children about the noises they hear when they go to bed at night. Can they describe the sounds? Explain that together they are going to write a story about the group's doll/teddy who finds it difficult to get to sleep. Discuss who else might be in the story.

On the flip chart begin to write the new story, writing just one sentence per page. Encourage children to suggest their own ideas as well as those in the book by Jill Murphy. Once the story has been written, read it back to the children. Do they like it? Are there any

changes that could be made to improve it? Once children are satisfied, give each child one page to illustrate and divide into smaller groups.

Activity: The keeper of the keys

Learning opportunity: Moving quietly with control. Collaborating to play a circle game.

Early Learning Goal: Physical Development. Children will be able to move with control and co-ordination.

Resources: Large bunch of keys.

Key vocabulary: Quietly, slowly, keys, blindfold, guard.

Organisation: Whole group.

What to do:

After a warm-up activity which encourages children to listen, arrange them sitting on the floor in a large circle. Show everyone the keys. Ask the children to shut their eyes and listen to the sound the keys make as they are picked up. Ask if anyone thinks they could pick them up without making a sound. Allow two children to demonstrate.

Pick a child to be 'The keeper of the keys' and to sit on a chair placed in the middle of the circle. Explain that the keeper has to guard the keys. If they hear someone approaching the keys they should point to where the sound is coming from. If they point at the person they have saved the keys. If someone manages to take the keys back to their place without being pointed at, the keys are lost. The keeper may only point five times. Explain that when everyone is sitting silently you will pick someone to try and take the keys.

Talk about the need to sit very still and, when picked, to move very slowly and quietly. When everyone has understood the game, blindfold the keeper and play until all children have had the chance to be either the keeper or the taker. The game can be extended by having more than one taker at a time and by reducing the number of points allowed to three.

Display

Display the instruments which children have made on a table. On another table put out a selection of instruments along with *Mr Little's Noisy Car*, *Peace at Last*, the group's own big book and other well-known picture books. Encourage pairs of children to use the instruments during independent activity times to make sound effects for the stories.

Week 4

Looking week

Personal, Social and Emotional Development

- Encourage children to take turns whilst playing 'I spy'. Clues could be by colour, initial sound or position. (PS8)

- Play blindfold games. (PS6, 8)

Communication, Language and Literacy

- Share books such as *I Spy Schooldays: a Book of Picture Riddles* by Walter Wick and Jean Marzollo (Scholastic) or *1001 Things to Spot on the Farm* by Gillian Doherty (Usborne) which encourage children to look closely at the pictures, to use descriptive vocabulary and to discuss with others as objects are found or cannot be seen. (L7)

- Encourage children to practise letter formation by making eye charts for the role play area. (L19)

- Read *If at first you do not see* by Ruth Brown. Talk about what is in each picture. Does everyone see the same things? (L5)

Mathematical Development

- Count how many children have each eye colour. Display the results as a bar chart (see activity opposite) (M1, 4)

- Provide each child with a book made from two pieces of A4 paper folded in half. On each page write a number from one to five. Give each child a number of magazines/catalogues which have people in them and ask the children to cut out faces and stick the given number on each page. Use the books for counting and for

introducing the idea of doubles - if there are two faces on a page there will be four eyes or two pairs. (M2, 3)

- Help children to make spectacles for a teddy bear out of pipe cleaners and to talk about the shapes used for the eye pieces. Can children make square eye pieces? What would triangular ones look like? (M9)

Knowledge and Understanding of the World

- Invite an adult who wears glasses to talk to the group about their glasses and what happens when they go to the optician. (K8)

- Talk about eyes and what eyelashes and eyebrows are for. Encourage children to notice the variety in eye colours and that all eyes are different even though many people have blue, brown, grey and green eyes. (K2, 3)

- Enjoy playing with safe kaleidoscopes and periscopes. (K1, 4)

Physical Development

- Talk about the importance of looking when playing with balls and bats. Allow free play, encouraging children always to keep their eyes on the ball. (PD6)

- Play a variety of aiming games such as skittles or throwing bean bags or balls into hoops or buckets. (PD6)

- Play a game where a coloured card is used to signify an action such as jump, walk or hop. Encourage children to keep a close eye on the colour card and to change their action immediately the cards have been changed. (PD2, 3)

Creative Development

- During free painting, encourage children to look closely at shapes and colours. (C4)

- Cut out pairs of spectacle frames from card and let children decorate them with sequins and other shiny and bright materials. Put them on sale in the optician role play area. (C1)

- Set up the role play area as an optician's with letter charts. Invite children to test friends', dolls' and teddy bears' eyes (see activity opposite). (C4)

Activity: Eye-colour bar chart

Learning opportunity: Collaborating to make a bar chart and comparing the number of children with different eye colours.

Early Learning Goal: Mathematical Development. Children will be able to say and use number names and use language such as 'more' or 'less' to compare two numbers.

Resources: Plastic mirrors; eyes cut from white paper; crayons in eye colours; a noticeboard with axes and labels for the bar chart at child height (see diagram); Blu-tack.

Key vocabulary: Bar chart, colours for eye colours, numbers sufficient to count the eyes, more, less.

Organisation: Whole group.

What to do:

Whilst sitting in a circle on the floor talk about eye colours. Ask children in turn to as their eye colour. Where children are

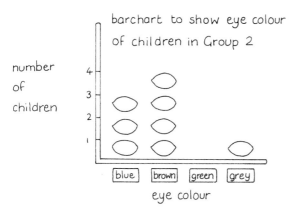

uncertain provide a mirror for them to check. Show the group the cut out eyes. Explain that they will be used to make a record of their eye colours. Invite children in turn to select a crayon the same colour as their eyes and to go and colour their iris. Once coloured help children to stick their eye on the prepared bar chart. As a group use the bar chart to count how many children have each eye colour. Which colour of eye do most children have? Do more children have blue or brown eyes?

Activity: Optician role play area

Learning opportunity: Playing collaboratively in a role play situation.

Early Learning Goal: Creative Development. Children will be able to use their imagination in imaginative and role play.

Resources: A role play area set out as an optician's with: a white coat/shirt; a telephone; a diary; a selection of toy spectacles; plastic sun spectacles and home made spectacles; a mirror; a letter chart; a till.

Key vocabulary: Spectacles, glasses, eye test.

Organisation: Whole group introduction with small groups using the area.

What to do:

Involve children in the setting up of the optician's. Let them make eye testing charts and spectacles. Introduce the area to the whole group and talk about the items in it. Talk about the way an optician tests eyesight and the importance of helping customers to buy spectacles that they will be happy to wear. Choose a small group to play in the optician's and over the coming days encourage all children to take on a variety of roles.

Display

Mount and display the children's paintings as an art gallery. Number the pictures and make a catalogue of titles suggested by the children.

Around the bar chart place question cards which encourage children to extract information. Ask how many children have each eye colour. Which colour do most children have? Near the role play area display the spectacles made by children with price labels and a mirror.

Week 5

Healthy week

Personal, Social and Emotional Development

- Talk about the importance of wearing the right types of clothes when playing outside during different times of the year. This can help to keep us healthy (see activity opposite). (PS10)

- Read *Oliver's Fruit Salad* by Vivian French (Hodder Children's Books) or/and *Oliver's Vegetables*. Talk about favourite foods. (PS2, 3, 4)

- Read *Sports Day* by Nick Butterworth and Mick Inkpen (Picture Knight). Talk about the importance of keeping fit. Encourage children to play active games during play times. (PS4)

Communication, Language and Literacy

- Set up the role play area as a healthy eating cafe. (L1, 4)

- Read *The Shopping Basket* by John Burningham. (Red Fox). Which foods in the story would have been good to eat? Ask children to retell the story using the pictures as a reminder of events. (L3, 6, 9)

- Make picture or word menus for the cafe. (L16, 18, 19)

Mathematical Development

- Provide each child with a cut-out of a shopping basket and a list of healthy foods for them to draw in their basket (for example, 4 apples, 2 carrots, 3 beakers of water). (M2, 3)

- Repeat the basket activity but this time draw in the foods and ask children to write on a shopping list how many there are of each. (M2, 3)

- Buy and sell food in the role play cafe. (M5, 11)

Knowledge and Understanding of the World

- Having first checked for children's food allergies, try taste testing for a variety of fruits and raw vegetables. (K1, 3)

- Talk about the kinds of foods which are good to eat. Provide each child with a sandwich box made from a piece of A4 card folded in half. Ask children to make healthy packed lunches either by cutting pictures out of magazines or by drawing. (K3)

- Talk about places in the local environment where children enjoy playing and ones which are disliked. Talk about safety, why the places are liked or disliked and how children might like to change them. (K11)

Physical Development

- Talk about the importance of gradually using different parts of our bodies in a warm-up before doing an activity which involves a lot of movement. Do a 'follow my leader' warm-up and talk about which parts of the body are being used (see activity opposite). (PD2, 4)

- Set up a variety of challenges which involve both fine motor and gross motor skills. Examples include spooning water from one container to another, threading beads, stacking cubes, catching a ball, dribbling a ball, jumping, skipping. Repeat these activities a number of times over the week and show children how practice can help us to improve. (PD6)

- Make healthy foods from playdough. (PD8)

Creative Development

- On paper plates use tissue paper to make a healthy meal. (C1)

- Weave place mats for the healthy cafe. (C1)

- Print with vegetables and hard fruits. (C1)

Activity: Warming Up

Learning opportunity: Moving with control and following instructions.

Early Learning Goal: Physical Development. Children will be able to move with control and co-ordination. They will recognise the importance of keeping healthy and things which contribute to this.

Resources: Large space.

Key vocabulary: Circle, fast, slow, quietly, parts of the body.

Organisation: Whole group.

What to do:

Sitting on the floor, talk to children about the importance of gradually warming up before they begin very active activities and games. Hold up a hand and ask children which parts can move. Do a variety of finger and wrist exercises and ask children to copy. Gradually continue with other parts of the body, encouraging children to recognise which parts are being exercised. Once all parts have been warmed up, play a favourite whole group game which involves running. Finally, cool down by playing sleeping lions where children lie on the ground as if asleep.

Activity: Wearing the right clothes

Learning opportunity: Picking and wearing clothes to suit a variety of weather conditions and temperatures.

Early Learning Goal: Personal, Social and Emotional Development. Children will dress and undress independently.

Resources: A large box containing a variety of items of clothing including ones for winter, wet and sunny weather such as a scarf, wellington boots, a sun hat and a raincoat; pictures of people dressed sensibly for a variety of weathers.

Key vocabulary: Names of clothing in the basket, wet, hot, cold, sunny, rainy, summer, winter.

Organisation: Whole group.

What to do:

Show the pictures of the people. Ask children what the people are wearing and why the items of clothing would be sensible ones to wear. Show the group the clothes that are in the basket. Ask a child to come and pick something which would be good to wear on a sunny day and to put it on. Ask why it would be good. What else would be useful on a sunny day? Repeat the activity for a variety of weathers and times of year. Encourage children to dress independently and to think of safety issues as well as the weather. For example, it would not be sensible to wear mittens if playing on a climbing frame. On a sunny day children should wear sun screen as well as a sun hat.

Display

On a large board put up a paper tablecloth and make a picnic display with the paper plates of healthy foods. Display the playdough foods on a table in front.

On a second board, stick up the pictures showing people in a variety of clothing and place the basket of clothes nearby. Invite children to enjoy wearing them as they visit the healthy cafe and for their own choice of role-play situations.

Week 6

Faces

Personal, Social and Emotional Development

- Talk about the 'Disguises day' which will take place at the end of the week and the jobs which will have to be done. (PS1, 2, 3)

- In circle time, talk about the importance of smiling. At the end of the session pass a smile around the circle (see activity opposite). (PS4, 6)

- Declare a 'Smile week' in which children will try to make people feel happy by smiling at them. (PS4, 6)

Communication, Language and Literacy

- Read *All Kinds of People* by Emma Damon (Tango Books). (L6)

- Provide children with paper and magazines from which to cut out smiling faces to make 'Smile please!' posters. (L16, 19)

- Talk about the way our faces can show how we are feeling. Ask children to show you a sad face, a happy face, a sleeping face, an angry face and a frightened face. Make small books which have a face on the cover crying or smiling and inside have sentences beginning with either 'I am sad when ....' or 'I am happy when ....' (L12, 18, 19)

Mathematical Development

- Use the face as the stimulus for counting activities with a small group. Count how many ears, eyes, noses and mouths the group has. Encourage them to notice that the number of eyes is the same as the number of ears. As children begin to notice similarities, ask them to predict how many chins the group will have. (M2, 11)

- Provide children with drawings of half faces. Encourage children to complete the pictures to make symmetrical faces. Use plastic mirrors to check the faces are symmetrical. (M9, 10)

- Provide each child with a selection of sticky paper regular shapes. Ask them to make pictures of faces. Encourage the children to talk about the shapes they use for the eyes, nose, mouth and ears. (M10)

Knowledge and Understanding of the World

- Use mirrors to allow children to observe their own faces and then make paper-plate face masks. (K2, 3)

- Give descriptions of children to the group and ask them to say who you are describing. As you play, help children to realise the differences and similarities they have with peers. (K3)

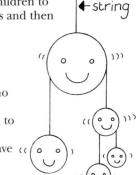

- Make happy face mobiles by cutting card faces, decorating both sides and stringing them together (see diagram). (K5)

Physical Development

- Tell the story of a spy putting on his disguise and encourage children to mime to the story. (PD1)

- Play shadow games in which children are the spies who are trying to track you. Stress the importance of only moving when you move and trying to keep in your shadow. (PD 1, 2)

- Draw with chalk on the playground a variety of large faces with flowing hair. Use them for aiming games and for walking on the lines. (PD1, 2)

Creative Development

- Sing 'If you're happy and you know it clap your hands' in *Apusskido Songs for Children* (A & C Black). (C5)

- Make two-faced clown puppets which smile and cry from paper plates (see activity opposite). (C1, 4)

- Use pasta, string and wool to make collages of faces. These are particularly effective if they are sprayed with silver or gold paint when dry. (C1)

Activity: Smiling

Learning opportunity: Working collaboratively, listening to others and talking with feeling.

Early Learning Goal: Personal, Social and Emotional Development. Children will be aware of their own needs, views and feelings and be sensitive to the needs, views and feelings of others. They will be responsive to significant experiences, showing a range of feelings including joy.

Resources: A hand puppet.

Key vocabulary: Smile, happy.

Organisation: Whole group sitting on the floor in a circle.

What to do:

Remind the group of the routines for circle time and the importance of always looking at the person who is speaking. Praise those who are already looking at you as you talk.

Show the group your puppet. Tell the group its name and that it is very special to you because whenever you see it you smile. Ask the children how they feel when someone smiles at them. What makes them smile?

Pass the puppet around the circle. Whoever holds the puppet has the opportunity to speak. Once all the children who want to have spoken, talk about the importance of smiles for helping us to feel good. Finish by 'passing a smile' around the circle.

Activity: Clown puppets

Learning opportunity: Using a variety of materials to make puppets and using the puppets in imaginative, role play situations.

Early Learning Goal: Creative Development. Children will be able to explore colour and form. They will use their imagination in imaginative and role play.

Resources: Selection of scraps of material, paper, wool, sequins; felt pens; ready mixed paints; glue; scissors; an example of a paper-plate puppet clown. For each child: two small paper plates, two card triangles from which to make the hat and a thick 30cm long piece of dowelling or cardboard tubing.

Key vocabulary: Names of materials and colours being used, clown, happy, sad.

Organisation: Small group.

What to do:

Show the group the example of the clown puppet. Show them that it has two faces and ask why that would be useful in a play. Let the group ask the clown some questions.

Give each child a plate and ask them to draw a happy face on the underneath/non waxy side. Remind children of where they need to position the eyes. Repeat this with the sad face. Finally, stick strips of paper or wool on for hair. When dry, stick the plates together with glue with the dowelling/card tube stuck inside for the neck/handle. (See diagram.)

Decorate the card triangles brightly and glue them on to the head. When completely dry, the children can use their puppets to make plays to perform for their friends.

Display

Display the face collages with a 'Smile please' poster on a board and hang the smiling mobiles close by. Cover a table with a drape and carefully place the clown puppets on it. To the side arrange a table or large box as a puppet theatre for children to use their puppets in. Also include a book of tickets and till so that children can sell tickets for their shows.

Bringing it all together

A day of disguises

Explain to the children that they are going to have 'A day of disguises'. They will learn how to disguise themselves. At the end there will be a special disguise parade to which parents and friends will be invited to come.

The event will work best if it is held in a large room/hall where a variety of activities can be set out for children to visit in turn. Divide the children into small groups of about four children with an adult. Give each child a piece of card which is set out as a passport to be completed during the event. Allocate each group to an activity and explain the direction in which they will move. Make sure that the adults have ideas for games such as 'I spy' which they could play with their group should an activity finish before it is time to move on. If enough adults are available it is useful to have each activity run by a different person whilst others move round with the children.

Activities

- Having first checked that children are not allergic to face paints, invite adults to come in and help give children a new look.

- Put out passport photograph sized pieces of paper and crayons for children to record their new face and stick it in the passport.

- Talk to children about the way people can often be recognised from a long way off by how they move. Challenge the children to try walking in a variety of ways as if they were someone else. Help them to practise the walk they will use in the disguise parade.

- Talk to children about their names and their ages. For their disguise they will need a new name and age. Help children to record these in their passports.

- Make a collection of clothes which children can dress up in for their disguise. Collect enough for children to be able to keep the clothes on for the whole event.

- Use an ink pad to record children's thumb and finger prints.

- Talk about clothes and the way we often recognise people from the things they wear. Make a collection of shoes owned by children in the group. Play a game in which children have to recognise their own shoes and then identify those of friends. Before playing, check that all shoes are named but cover the names up for the game.

- Give each child a sheet containing nine outlines of identical faces. Invite the children to add lines to disguise the faces.

- Invite a parent with a Polaroid camera to take instant photos of the complete disguise for the passports.

Food

Although food is not a requirement for a 'disguises event' most children and adults will enjoy some refreshments after the parade.

Involve the children in preparing food:

- Make face biscuits by using melted chocolate, icing tubes and sweets to decorate plain biscuits.

- Make a 'disguised cocktail' by mixing a selection of fruit juices and adding small pieces of cut-up soft fruits. Can children identify which fruits and juices are in the cocktail?

The parade

After all the disguise activities have been done, ask children to sit on the floor in a circle. Arrange chairs around the circle for parents and friends. Put on some quiet, background music to which children will enjoy parading, such as the theme music to the *Pink Panther*. Invite children in turn to tell everyone their new name and age, and to walk around the circle in role. Once all those who want to parade have done so, share the biscuits and fruit cocktail.

Resources

Resources to collect

- Pictures of faces from magazines.
- Sequins.
- Plastic mirrors.
- Kaleidoscopes.
- Periscopes.
- Clothes for making disguises.

Everyday resources

- Boxes, large and small for modelling.
- Papers and cards of different weights, colours and textures available, such as sugar paper, corrugated card, silver and shiny papers.
- Dry powder paints for mixing and mixed paints for covering large areas such as card tree trunks.
- Different sized paint brushes from household brushes to thin brushes for delicate work and a variety of paint mixing containers.
- A variety of drawing and colouring pencils, crayons, pastels, charcoals, chalks.
- Additional decorative and finishing materials such as sequins, foil, glitter, tinsel, shiny wool and threads, beads, pieces of textiles, parcel ribbon.
- Table covers.
- Pasta.

Stories

Skeleton Crew by Allan Ahlberg and Andre Amstutz (Mammoth).

Funnybones by Janet and Allan Ahlberg (Puffin Books).

Look into their Eyes by Richard Brassey (Dolphin).

If At First You Do Not See by Ruth Brown (Andersen Press).

The Shopping Basket by John Burningham (Red Fox).

Sports Day by Nick Butterworth and Mick Inkpen (Hodder Children's Books).

All Kinds of People by Emma Damon (Tango Books).

Oliver's Fruit Salad by Vivian French (Hodder Children's Books).

Oliver's Milk Shake by Vivian French (Hodder Children's Books).

Oliver's Vegetables by Vivian French (Hodder Children's Books).

Peace at Last by Jill Murphy (Macmillan Children's Books).

Don't do that! by Tony Ross (Red Fox).

I Don't Want to go to Bed by Julie Sykes and Tim Warnes (Magi Publications).

Non fiction

Feelings by Aliki (Morrow Avon - US).

1001 Things to Spot on the Farm by Gillian Doherty (Usborne).

Find out about the Body by Anita Ganeri (BBC).

I Know Where my Food goes by Jacqui Maynard (Walker Books).

First Encyclopedia of the Human Body by Richard Walker (Kingfisher).

Songs

Okki-tokki-unga Action Songs for Children chosen by Beatrice Harrop, Linda Friend and David Gadsby (A & C Black).

Apusskido Songs for Children chosen by Beatrice Harrop, Peggy Blakely and David Gadsby (A & C Black).

Poems

This Little Puffin by Elizabeth Matterson (Puffin).

Out and About by Shirley Hughes (Walker Books).

Collecting evidence of children's learning

Monitoring children's development is an important task. Keeping a record of children's achievements will help you to see progress and will draw attention to those who are having difficulties for some reason. If a child needs additional professional help, such as speech therapy, your records will provide valuable evidence.

Records should be the result of collaboration between group leaders, parents and carers. Parents should be made aware of your record keeping policies when their child joins your group. Show them the type of records you are keeping and make sure they understand that they have an opportunity to contribute. As a general rule, your records should form an open document. Any parent should have access to records relating to his or her child. Take regular opportunities to talk to parents about children's progress. If you have formal discussions regarding children about whom you have particular concerns, a dated record of the main points should be kept.

Keeping it manageable

Records should be helpful in informing group leaders, adult helpers and parents and always be for the benefit of the child. However, keeping records of every aspect of each child's development can become a difficult task. The sample shown will help to keep records manageable and useful. The golden rule is to keep them simple.

Observations will basically fall into three categories:

- **Spontaneous records:** Sometimes you will want to make a note of observations as they happen, for example, a child is heard counting cars accurately during a play activity, or is seen to play collaboratively for the first time.

- **Planned observations:** Sometimes you will plan to make observations of children's developing skills in their everyday activities. Using the learning opportunity identified for an activity will help you to make appropriate judgements about children's capabilities and to record them systematically.

To collect information:

- talk to children about their activities and listen to their responses;

- listen to children talking to each other;

- observe children's work such as early writing, drawings, paintings and 3D models. (Keeping photocopies or photographs is useful.)

Sometimes you may wish to set up 'one off' activities for the purposes of monitoring development. Some pre-school groups, for example, ask children to make a drawing of themselves at the beginning of each term to record their progressing skills in both co-ordination and observation. Do not attempt to make records after every activity!

- **Reflective observations:** It is useful to spend regular time reflecting on the progress of a few children (about four each week). Aim to make some brief comments about each child every half term.

Informing your planning

Collecting evidence about children's progress is time consuming and it is important that it is useful. When you are planning, use the information you have collected to help you to decide what learning opportunities you need to provide next for children. For example, a child who has poor pencil or brush control will benefit from more play with dough or construction toys to build the strength of hand muscles.

Example of recording chart

Name: Jonathan Hogg		D.O.B. 18.2.97		Date of entry: 13.9.00	
Term	**Personal, Social and Emotional Development**	**Communication, Language and Literacy**	**Mathematical Development**	**Knowledge and Understanding of the World**	**Physical Development**	**Creative Development**
ONE	Reluctant to say good bye to mother. Prefers adult company 20.9.00 EMH	Enjoys listening to stories, particularly liked *Funnybones*. Can write first name. Good pencil control 20.11.00 EMH	Is able to say numbers to ten and count accurately five objects. Recognises and names squares and circles. 5.11.00 BM	Keen to ask questions. Is fascinated by all facts about the body. 16.10.00 AC	Can balance on one leg. Loved trying to walk in different ways. Does not like the feel of playdough. 16.10.00 AC	Made a wonderful face collage. Enjoys painting, particularly mixing own colours. 20.10.00 LSS
TWO						
THREE						

Skills overview of six week plan

Week	Topic focus	Personal, Social and Emotional Development	Communication Language and Literacy	Mathematical Development	Knowledge and Understanding of the World	Physical Development	Creative Development
1	Bits and pieces	Appreciating body parts	Listening Writing Book making	Comparative language Counting	Labelling body parts Constructing	Moving with control and imagination	Singing Painting Making sounds
2	Handy week	Listening to others; Taking turns; Developing independence	Describing Writing	Counting Comparing size Estimating	Making observations Comparing Describing	Catching Throwing Using malleable materials	Finger painting Singing
3	Listening week	Sensitivity to others safety Listening	Listening to stories Making a book Initial sounds; Rhyming	Comparative language; Shape Counting	Comparing similarities and differences	Moving with control and imagination	Dancing Playing instruments; Singing
4	Looking week	Taking turns	Using descriptive vocabulary; Letter formation	Language of shape Counting	Talking Investigating Observing	Aiming Moving with awareness of space	Using materials Painting Role play
5	Healthy week	Health awareness	Talking Purposeful writing Discussing	Counting Using money	Using senses Environmental preferences	Moving with control; Using malleable materials	Weaving Collage
6	Faces	Expressing emotions Collaborative planning	Listening to a story Writing for a purpose Taling about feelings	Shape awareness Counting Symmetry	Observing Describing Using materials	Moving with imagination and control	Singing Collage Using tools

Home links

The theme of All About Me lends itself to useful links with children's homes and families. Through working together children and adults gain respect for each other and build comfortable and confident relationships.

Establishing partnerships

- Keep parents informed about the topic of All About Me and the themes for each week. By understanding the work of the group, parents will enjoy the involvement of contributing ideas, time and resources.

- Photocopy the parent's page for each child to take home.

- Invite friends, childminders and families to share all or part of the 'Day of disguises'.

Visiting enthusiasts

- Invite adults to come in to talk about wearing spectacles and contact lenses.

- Invite adults who enjoy face painting to run an activity at sthe disguises event.

Resource requests

- Ask parents to contribute clothes which are no longer needed for making disguises.

- Parcel bows, wrapping papers, wall papers and any interesting boxes and packaging are invaluable for collage work and a wide range of interesting activities.

The day of disguises

- It is always useful to have extra adults at times such as the disguises event.

- Put out a suggestion box in which parents can contribute ideas for activities which could be used on the day of disguises.

- Invite parents to donate games such as 'Misfits' which fit with the disguises theme.